COMMON ABBREVIATIONS

D1760453

alt	Alternate		**rev St st**	
beg	Begin/beginning		**RH**	
bet	Between		**rnd**	Round
BO	Bind off		**RS**	Right side
CC	Contrasting color		**SKP**	Slip, knit, pass: slip 1 knitwise, knit 1, pass slip stitch over knit stitch
cn	Cable needle			
CO	Cast on			
cont	Continue		**SK2P**	Slip 1 knitwise, knit 2 together, pass slip stitch over knit 2 together
dec	Decrease			
dpn	Double-pointed needles			
inc	Increase		**sl**	Slip
K	Knit		**sl1k**	Slip 1 knitwise
k2tog	Knit 2 stitches together		**sl1p**	Slip 1 purlwise
kwise	Knitwise		**slst**	Slip stitch(es)
LH	Lefthand		**ssk**	Slip, slip, knit (a decrease)
lp	Loop		**ssp**	Slip, slip, purl (a decrease)
M1	Make 1 (increase a stitch)		**sssk**	Slip, slip, slip, knit (a double decrease)
M1L	Make 1 left			
M1R	Make 1 right		**st**	Stitch
MC	Main color		**St st**	Stockinette stitch
p	Purl		**tbl**	Though back loop(s)
p2tog	Purl 2 stitches together		**tog**	Together
pat/patt	Pattern		**WS**	Wrong side
pm	Place marker		**wyib**	With yarn in back
prev	Previous		**wyif**	With yarn in front
psso	Pass slipped stitch over		**yb**	Yarn back
rem	Remaining		**yf/yfwd**	Yarn forward
rep	Repeat		**yo**	Yarn over
			yon	Yarn over needle
			yrn	Yarn round needle

KEEP
CALM
— AND —
CAST ON

This journal

HOLDS THE PLANS, WORKS IN PROGRESS,
AND FIBER–BASED DREAMS OF:

_____

If found,

PLEASE CONTACT:

_____

_____

_____

FAVORITE SOURCES

Use this space to note addresses, websites, store hours, and phone numbers of your favorite sources for patterns and supplies.

YARN STASH

	YARN	NUMBER OF SKEINS	MAKER/FIBER
1			
2			
3			
4			
5			
6			
7			

May each skein find the perfect project,
yet may your stash never run too low.

COLOR/ DYE LOT	WEIGHT	SOURCE	COST	NOTES

YARN STASH

	YARN	NUMBER OF SKEINS	MAKER/FIBER
8			
9			
10			
11			
12			
13			
14			

All you knit is love.

COLOR/ DYE LOT	WEIGHT	SOURCE	COST	NOTES

YARN STASH

	YARN	NUMBER OF SKEINS	MAKER/FIBER
15			
16			
17			
18			
19			
20			
21			

Homemade gifts contain the talent of your hands and the love of your heart.

COLOR/ DYE LOT	WEIGHT	SOURCE	COST	NOTES

YARN STASH

	YARN	NUMBER OF SKEINS	MAKER/FIBER
22			
23			
24			
25			
26			
27			
28			

Everyone can see yarn;
knitters see potential.

COLOR/ DYE LOT	WEIGHT	SOURCE	COST	NOTES

YARN
STASH

	YARN	NUMBER OF SKEINS	MAKER/FIBER
29			
30			
31			
32			
33			
34			
35			

Life is short.
Knit with the fancy yarn.

COLOR/ DYE LOT	WEIGHT	SOURCE	COST	NOTES

YARN STASH

	YARN	NUMBER OF SKEINS	MAKER/FIBER
36			
37			
38			
39			
40			
41			
42			

Home is where the yarn stash is.

COLOR/DYE LOT	WEIGHT	SOURCE	COST	NOTES

PROJECT

_____

_____ _____
KNITTED FOR   DATE

YARN

Number of Skeins	Maker/Fiber	Color/ Dye Lot	Weight/Length	Gauge

Needles:	Finished Size:
Notions:	Pattern Source:

PROJECT

_____

_____   _____
KNITTED FOR   DATE

YARN

Number of Skeins	Maker/Fiber	Color/ Dye Lot	Weight/Length	Gauge

Needles:	Finished Size:
Notions:	Pattern Source:

PROJECT

_____

_____   _____
KNITTED FOR   DATE

YARN				
Number of Skeins	Maker/Fiber	Color/ Dye Lot	Weight/Length	Gauge

Needles:	Finished Size:
Notions:	Pattern Source:

PROJECT

_____

KNITTED FOR _____   DATE _____

YARN

Number of Skeins	Maker/Fiber	Color/ Dye Lot	Weight/Length	Gauge

Needles:	Finished Size:
Notions:	Pattern Source:

PROJECT

_____

_____   _____

KNITTED FOR   DATE

YARN

Number of Skeins	Maker/Fiber	Color/ Dye Lot	Weight/Length	Gauge

Needles:	Finished Size:
Notions:	Pattern Source:

PROJECT

_____

_____   _____
KNITTED FOR   DATE

YARN

Number of Skeins	Maker/Fiber	Color/ Dye Lot	Weight/Length	Gauge

Needles:	Finished Size:
Notions:	Pattern Source:

PROJECT

_____

_____   _____

KNITTED FOR   DATE

YARN

Number of Skeins	Maker/Fiber	Color/ Dye Lot	Weight/Length	Gauge

Needles:	Finished Size:
Notions:	Pattern Source:

PROJECT

_____

_____   _____
KNITTED FOR   DATE

YARN

Number of Skeins	Maker/Fiber	Color/Dye Lot	Weight/Length	Gauge

Needles:	Finished Size:
Notions:	Pattern Source:

PROJECT

_____

_____ _____

KNITTED FOR   DATE

YARN

Number of Skeins	Maker/Fiber	Color/ Dye Lot	Weight/Length	Gauge

Needles:	Finished Size:
Notions:	Pattern Source:

PROJECT

_____

_____   _____
KNITTED FOR   DATE

YARN

Number of Skeins	Maker/Fiber	Color/Dye Lot	Weight/Length	Gauge

Needles:	Finished Size:
Notions:	Pattern Source:

PROJECT

_____

_____   _____
KNITTED FOR   DATE

YARN				
Number of Skeins	Maker/Fiber	Color/ Dye Lot	Weight/Length	Gauge

Needles:	Finished Size:
Notions:	Pattern Source:

PROJECT

_____

_____   _____

KNITTED FOR   DATE

YARN

Number of Skeins	Maker/Fiber	Color/ Dye Lot	Weight/Length	Gauge

Needles:	Finished Size:
Notions:	Pattern Source:

PROJECT

_____

_____   _____

KNITTED FOR   DATE

YARN

Number of Skeins	Maker/Fiber	Color/ Dye Lot	Weight/Length	Gauge

Needles:	Finished Size:
Notions:	Pattern Source:

PROJECT

_____

_____ _____

KNITTED FOR   DATE

YARN

Number of Skeins	Maker/Fiber	Color/ Dye Lot	Weight/Length	Gauge

Needles:	Finished Size:
Notions:	Pattern Source:

PROJECT

_____

_____   _____

KNITTED FOR   DATE

YARN

Number of Skeins	Maker/Fiber	Color/ Dye Lot	Weight/Length	Gauge

Needles:	Finished Size:
Notions:	Pattern Source:

PROJECT

_____

_____   _____
KNITTED FOR   DATE

YARN

Number of Skeins	Maker/Fiber	Color/ Dye Lot	Weight/Length	Gauge

Needles:	Finished Size:
Notions:	Pattern Source:

PROJECT

_____

_____   _____
KNITTED FOR   DATE

YARN

Number of Skeins	Maker/Fiber	Color/ Dye Lot	Weight/Length	Gauge

Needles:	Finished Size:
Notions:	Pattern Source:

PROJECT

_____

_____   _____

KNITTED FOR   DATE

YARN

Number of Skeins	Maker/Fiber	Color/ Dye Lot	Weight/Length	Gauge

Needles:	Finished Size:
Notions:	Pattern Source:

PROJECT

_____

_____   _____
KNITTED FOR   DATE

YARN

Number of Skeins	Maker/Fiber	Color/ Dye Lot	Weight/Length	Gauge

Needles:	Finished Size:
Notions:	Pattern Source:

PROJECT

_____

_____   _____
KNITTED FOR   DATE

YARN				
Number of Skeins	Maker/Fiber	Color/ Dye Lot	Weight/Length	Gauge

Needles:	Finished Size:
Notions:	Pattern Source:

PROJECT

_____

_____   _____

KNITTED FOR   DATE

YARN

Number of Skeins	Maker/Fiber	Color/ Dye Lot	Weight/Length	Gauge

Needles:	Finished Size:
Notions:	Pattern Source:

PROJECT

_____

_____   _____
KNITTED FOR   DATE

YARN

Number of Skeins	Maker/Fiber	Color/ Dye Lot	Weight/Length	Gauge

Needles:	Finished Size:
Notions:	Pattern Source:

PROJECT

_____

_____   _____
KNITTED FOR   DATE

YARN				
Number of Skeins	Maker/Fiber	Color/ Dye Lot	Weight/Length	Gauge

Needles:	Finished Size:
Notions:	Pattern Source:

PROJECT

_____

_____   _____
KNITTED FOR   DATE

YARN

Number of Skeins	Maker/Fiber	Color/Dye Lot	Weight/Length	Gauge

Needles: Finished Size:

Notions: Pattern Source:

PROJECT

_____

_____   _____
KNITTED FOR   DATE

YARN

Number of Skeins	Maker/Fiber	Color/Dye Lot	Weight/Length	Gauge

Needles:	Finished Size:
Notions:	Pattern Source:

PROJECT

_____

_____ _____
KNITTED FOR   DATE

YARN

Number of Skeins	Maker/Fiber	Color/ Dye Lot	Weight/Length	Gauge

Needles:	Finished Size:
Notions:	Pattern Source:

PROJECT

_____

_____   _____
KNITTED FOR   DATE

YARN

Number of Skeins	Maker/Fiber	Color/ Dye Lot	Weight/Length	Gauge

Needles:	Finished Size:
Notions:	Pattern Source:

PROJECT

_____

_____   _____

KNITTED FOR   DATE

YARN

Number of Skeins	Maker/Fiber	Color/Dye Lot	Weight/Length	Gauge

Needles:	Finished Size:
Notions:	Pattern Source:

PROJECT

_____

_____ _____
KNITTED FOR   DATE

YARN

Number of Skeins	Maker/Fiber	Color/ Dye Lot	Weight/Length	Gauge

Needles:	Finished Size:
Notions:	Pattern Source:

PROJECT

_____

_____   _____

KNITTED FOR   DATE

YARN

Number of Skeins	Maker/Fiber	Color/ Dye Lot	Weight/Length	Gauge

Needles: Finished Size:

Notions: Pattern Source:

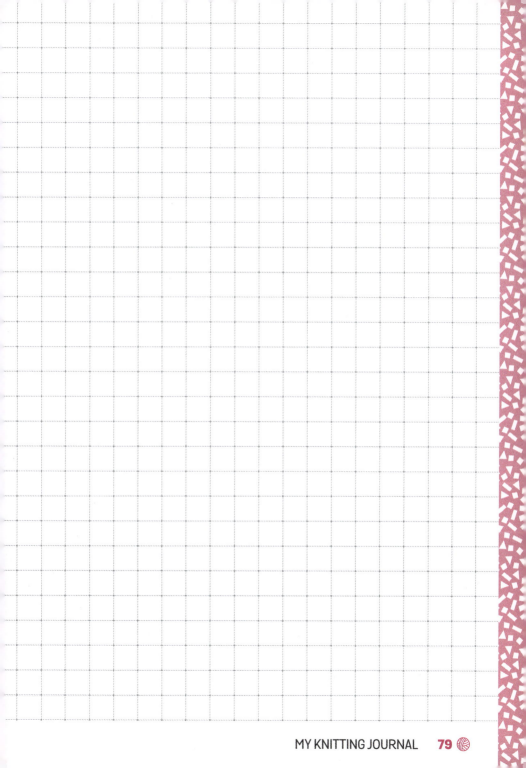

PROJECT

_____

_____ _____
KNITTED FOR   DATE

YARN

Number of Skeins	Maker/Fiber	Color/ Dye Lot	Weight/Length	Gauge

Needles:

Finished Size:

Notions:

Pattern Source:

PROJECT

_____

_____   _____
KNITTED FOR   DATE

YARN

Number of Skeins	Maker/Fiber	Color/ Dye Lot	Weight/Length	Gauge

Needles:

Finished Size:

Notions:

Pattern Source:

PROJECT

_____

_____   _____
KNITTED FOR   DATE

YARN

Number of Skeins	Maker/Fiber	Color/Dye Lot	Weight/Length	Gauge

Needles:	Finished Size:
Notions:	Pattern Source:

PROJECT

_____

_____ _____

KNITTED FOR   DATE

YARN

Number of Skeins	Maker/Fiber	Color/ Dye Lot	Weight/Length	Gauge

Needles:	Finished Size:
Notions:	Pattern Source:

PROJECT

_____

_____   _____
KNITTED FOR   DATE

YARN				
Number of Skeins	Maker/Fiber	Color/ Dye Lot	Weight/Length	Gauge

Needles:	Finished Size:
Notions:	Pattern Source:

PROJECT

_____

_____   _____
KNITTED FOR   DATE

YARN

Number of Skeins	Maker/Fiber	Color/ Dye Lot	Weight/Length	Gauge

Needles:	Finished Size:
Notions:	Pattern Source:

PROJECT

_____

_____ _____
KNITTED FOR   DATE

YARN

Number of Skeins	Maker/Fiber	Color/ Dye Lot	Weight/Length	Gauge

Needles:	Finished Size:
Notions:	Pattern Source:

PROJECT

_____

_____   _____

KNITTED FOR   DATE

YARN				
Number of Skeins	Maker/Fiber	Color/ Dye Lot	Weight/Length	Gauge

Needles:

Finished Size:

Notions:

Pattern Source:

PROJECT

_____

_____   _____
KNITTED FOR   DATE

YARN				
Number of Skeins	Maker/Fiber	Color/ Dye Lot	Weight/Length	Gauge

Needles:	Finished Size:
Notions:	Pattern Source:

PROJECT

_____

_____   _____
KNITTED FOR   DATE

YARN

Number of Skeins	Maker/Fiber	Color/Dye Lot	Weight/Length	Gauge

Needles:	Finished Size:
Notions:	Pattern Source:

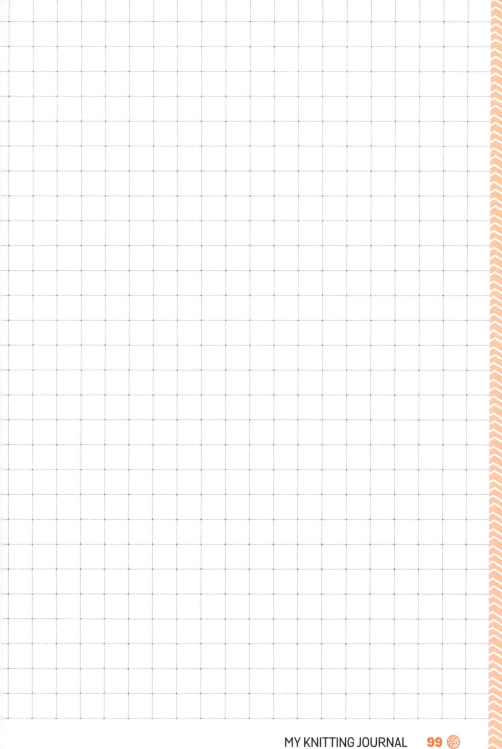

PROJECT

_____

_____   _____

KNITTED FOR   DATE

YARN

Number of Skeins	Maker/Fiber	Color/ Dye Lot	Weight/Length	Gauge

Needles:	Finished Size:
Notions:	Pattern Source:

PROJECT

_____

_____   _____

KNITTED FOR   DATE

YARN				
Number of Skeins	Maker/Fiber	Color/ Dye Lot	Weight/Length	Gauge

Needles:	Finished Size:
Notions:	Pattern Source:

PROJECT

_____

_____   _____
KNITTED FOR   DATE

YARN

Number of Skeins	Maker/Fiber	Color/ Dye Lot	Weight/Length	Gauge

Needles:

Finished Size:

Notions:

Pattern Source:

PROJECT

_____

_____   _____

KNITTED FOR   DATE

YARN				
Number of Skeins	Maker/Fiber	Color/ Dye Lot	Weight/Length	Gauge

Needles:	Finished Size:
Notions:	Pattern Source:

PROJECT

_____

_____   _____
KNITTED FOR   DATE

YARN

Number of Skeins	Maker/Fiber	Color/ Dye Lot	Weight/Length	Gauge

Needles:	Finished Size:
Notions:	Pattern Source:

PROJECT

_____

_____   _____
KNITTED FOR   DATE

YARN

Number of Skeins	Maker/Fiber	Color/ Dye Lot	Weight/Length	Gauge

Needles:	Finished Size:
Notions:	Pattern Source:

PROJECT

_____

_____ _____
KNITTED FOR   DATE

YARN

Number of Skeins	Maker/Fiber	Color/ Dye Lot	Weight/Length	Gauge

Needles:	Finished Size:
Notions:	Pattern Source:

PROJECT

_____

_____ _____
KNITTED FOR   DATE

YARN

Number of Skeins	Maker/Fiber	Color/Dye Lot	Weight/Length	Gauge

Needles:

Finished Size:

Notions:

Pattern Source:

PROJECT

_____

_____   _____
KNITTED FOR   DATE

YARN

Number of Skeins	Maker/Fiber	Color/ Dye Lot	Weight/Length	Gauge

Needles:	Finished Size:
Notions:	Pattern Source:

PROJECT

_____

_____ _____

KNITTED FOR   DATE

YARN

Number of Skeins	Maker/Fiber	Color/ Dye Lot	Weight/Length	Gauge

Needles: Finished Size:

Notions: Pattern Source:

PROJECT

_____

_____   _____

KNITTED FOR   DATE

YARN				
Number of Skeins	Maker/Fiber	Color/ Dye Lot	Weight/Length	Gauge

Needles:	Finished Size:
Notions:	Pattern Source:

PROJECT

_____

_____   _____

KNITTED FOR   DATE

YARN

Number of Skeins	Maker/Fiber	Color/ Dye Lot	Weight/Length	Gauge

Needles:	Finished Size:
Notions:	Pattern Source:

PROJECT

_____

_____ _____

KNITTED FOR   DATE

YARN				
Number of Skeins	Maker/Fiber	Color/ Dye Lot	Weight/Length	Gauge

Needles:	Finished Size:
Notions:	Pattern Source:

PROJECT

_____

_____   _____

KNITTED FOR   DATE

YARN

Number of Skeins	Maker/Fiber	Color/Dye Lot	Weight/Length	Gauge

Needles:	Finished Size:
Notions:	Pattern Source:

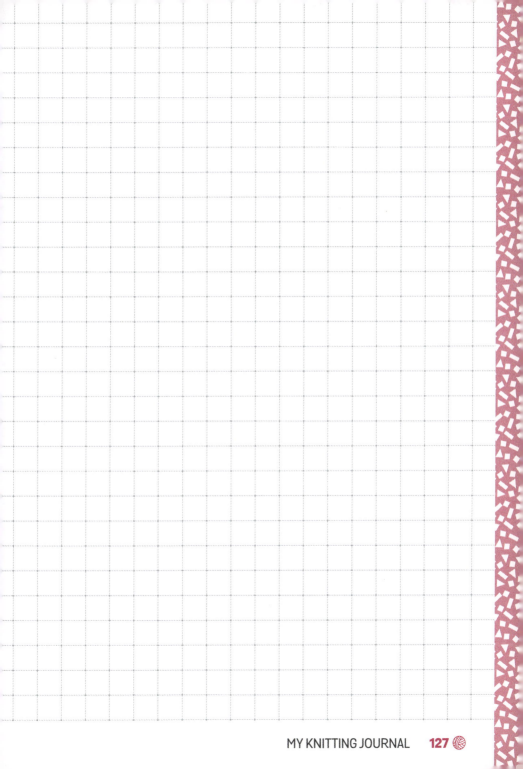

PROJECT

_____

_____   _____
KNITTED FOR   DATE

YARN

Number of Skeins	Maker/Fiber	Color/Dye Lot	Weight/Length	Gauge

Needles:	Finished Size:
Notions:	Pattern Source:

PROJECT

_____

_____ _____
KNITTED FOR   DATE

		YARN		
Number of Skeins	Maker/Fiber	Color/ Dye Lot	Weight/Length	Gauge

Needles:	Finished Size:
Notions:	Pattern Source:

PROJECT

_____

_____ _____

KNITTED FOR | DATE

YARN

Number of Skeins	Maker/Fiber	Color/ Dye Lot	Weight/Length	Gauge

Needles:	Finished Size:
Notions:	Pattern Source:

PROJECT

_____

_____   _____

KNITTED FOR   DATE

YARN				
Number of Skeins	Maker/Fiber	Color/ Dye Lot	Weight/Length	Gauge

Needles:	Finished Size:
Notions:	Pattern Source:

PROJECT

_____

_____   _____

KNITTED FOR   DATE

YARN				
Number of Skeins	Maker/Fiber	Color/ Dye Lot	Weight/Length	Gauge

Needles:	Finished Size:
Notions:	Pattern Source:

PROJECT

_____

_____   _____
KNITTED FOR   DATE

YARN

Number of Skeins	Maker/Fiber	Color/Dye Lot	Weight/Length	Gauge

Needles:	Finished Size:
Notions:	Pattern Source:

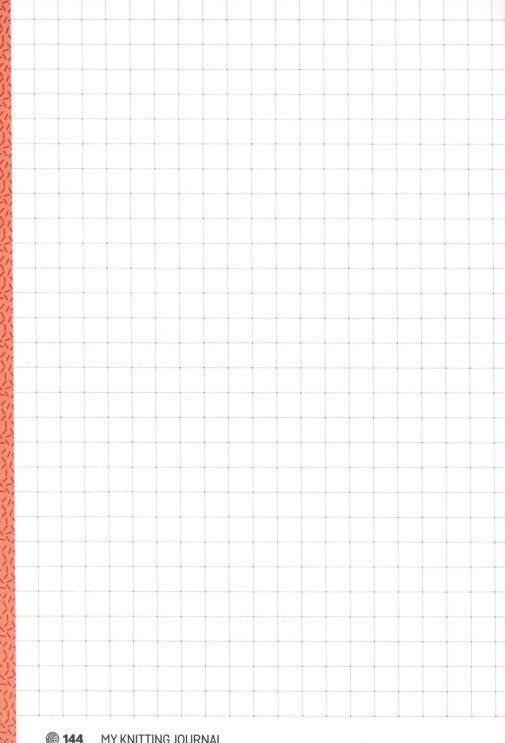

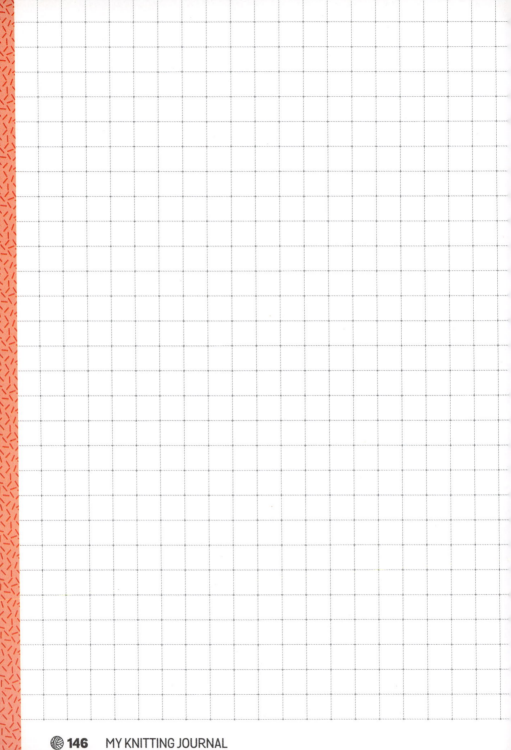

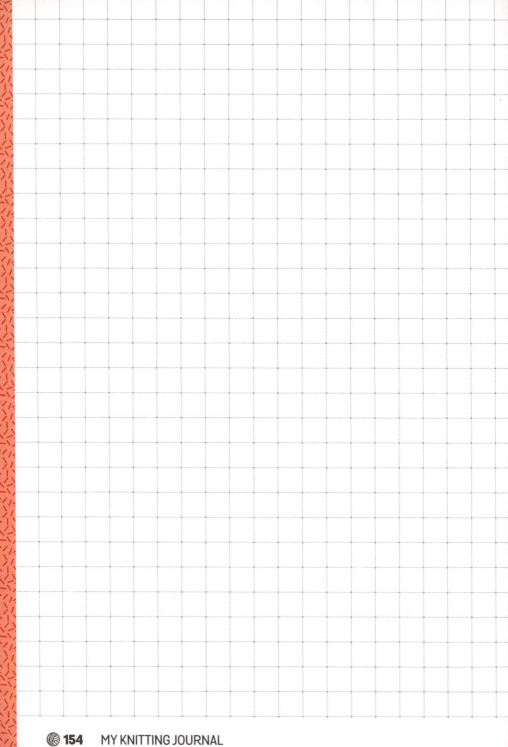

GO
FORTH
— AND —
KNIT

KNITTING NEEDLE CONVERSIONS

METRIC	US	UK
2mm	0	14
2.25mm	1	13
2.75mm	1	12
3mm	2	11
3.25mm	3	10
3.50mm	4	N/A
3.75mm	5	9
4mm	6	8
4.50mm	7	7
5mm	8	6
5.50mm	9	5
6mm	10	4
6.50mm	10 1/2	3
7mm	N/A	2
7.50mm	N/A	1
8mm	11	0
9mm	13	00
10mm	15	000
11mm	17	N/A
19mm	19	N/A
25mm	50	N/A

LAUNDRY SYMBOLS

 HAND WASH

 DO NOT WASH

 MACHINE WASH NORMAL

 MACHINE WASH PERM PRESS

 MACHINE WASH GENTLE

 DO NOT WRING

 MACHINE WASH COLD 80°F / 30°C

 MACHINE WASH WARM 105°F / 40°C

 MACHINE WASH HOT 120°F / 50°C

MACHINE WASH HOT 140°F / 60°C

MACHINE WASH HOT 160°F / 70°C

MACHINE WASH HOT 200°F / 95°C

 BLEACH

 DO NOT BLEACH

NON-CHLORINE BLEACH

HANG TO DRY

 DRIP DRY

 DRY FLAT

TUMBLE DRY NORMAL

 TUMBLE DRY PERM PRESS

 TUMBLE DRY GENTLE

TUMBLE DRY NO HEAT

TUMBLE DRY LOW HEAT

TUMBLE DRY HIGH HEAT

 IRON ANY TEMP STEAM OR DRY

IRON COOL HEAT REVERSE SIDE

IRON MEDIUM HEAT

IRON HIGH HEAT

 DO NOT IRON

 DO NOT STEAM

 DRY CLEAN

 DRY CLEAN ANY SOLVENT

 PETROLEUM SOLVENT ONLY

 DRY CLEAN LOW HEAT

 DRY CLEAN NO STEAM

 DO NOT DRY CLEAN

About the Author

Val Pierce's passion for knitting began when her father taught her to knit at the age of five. Later in life, she began home knitting for yarn manufacturers, and since then she has made a huge range of items, from evening dresses to teddy bears. She later began designing items of her own, and before long, her dreams were appearing in knitting and crochet magazines. She also teaches knitting and crochet to both adults and children.

Other Titles by Val Pierce

Love . . . Knitting

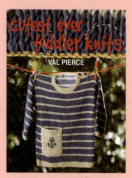

Cutest Ever Toddler Knits

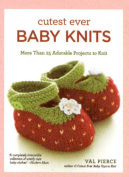

Cutest Ever Baby Knits

ISBN 978-1-64178-075-9

COPY PERMISSION: The written instructions, photographs, designs, patterns, and projects in this publication are intended for the personal use of the reader and may be reproduced for that purpose only. Any other use, especially commercial use, is forbidden under law without the written permission of the copyright holder.

NOTE: The use of products and trademark names is for informational purposes only, with no intention of infringement upon those trademarks.

Fox Chapel Publishing makes every effort to use environmentally friendly paper for printing.

© 2019 by Quiet Fox Designs, www.QuietFoxDesigns.com, an imprint of Fox Chapel Publishing Company, Inc., 903 Square Street, Mount Joy, PA 17552.

Charts entitled "Wraps per Inch (WPI) by Yarn Weight," "Yarn Weights," and "How to Measure" on the inner covers were provided by Craft Yarn Council (www.craftyarncouncil.com).

Images from Shutterstock.com: Melica (front cover); bosotochka (3 corners, 4–19 top and bottom borders, 20–139 patterned backgrounds and side borders, 140–157 side borders, back cover background); Nadiinko (2, 3–4 icons, 8–19 icons, 21–157 page number yarn ball, 158); Strejman (160 laundry symbols); and Alushka (back inner cover female drawing).

We are always looking for talented authors and artists. To submit an idea, please send a brief inquiry to acquisitions@foxchapelpublishing.com.

Printed in Singapore
First printing